THE P

JOHN SIDDIQUE

THE PRIZE

for Sue

Many thanks

John Siddique

A *The Rialto*
First Edition

ACKNOWLEDGEMENTS

Poems have appeared in the following magazines and anthologies *The Rialto, Fire, The Leeds Guide, Never Bury Poetry, Flux, The New Writer, Calabash, Kin, Gargoyle, Peace Poems, Redbeck Anthology of British South Asian Poetry, KISS, The Fire People.*

There are far too many people to thank for their support over the creation of this book, these are some but not all, Peter Kalu, Martin Glynn, Commonword, Michael Mackmin, Martin Colthorpe, Paula Truman, Allan Lloyd, Peter Arsecott, Shelia Staunton, Charles Bennett, Jack Mapanje, Julia Davis, Anna Goodman, Cherry Smyth, Jane Stubbs, Gary McKeone, Melanie Abrahams, Nadia Gilani, Rachel Feldberg, Tom Palmer. Special thanks to Juliette and James Barker for the loan of Ruddclough Barn in Cragg Vale, a beautiful retreat which inspired the 'Angelus' poems.

And of course without love we are nothing: Hannah Nunn, Kath Siddique, Chris Robinson, Stephen Hughes, John Holland, Xanthe Gresham, Sherry Robinson, Chris Howarth, Paul Dewhirst, Marie Evans. This book is dedicated to each of these people.

Many thanks to the Arts Council of England for advice, time and money.

J.S

First published in 2005
The Rialto PO Box 309 Aylsham Norwich England NR11 6LN

ISBN 0-9527444-8-1

The publisher acknowledges financial assistance from the Arts Council of England, East.

The Rialto is a Registered Charity No. 297553
Typeset in Perpetua 10 on 12.5pt
Design by Starfish, Norwich www.starfishlimited.com
Printed by Printing Services (Norwich) Limited

For the loved, the missing, and the dead.

CONTENTS

HORSEBONES

Last night the sky was obliterated.

Last night your mouth said one thing
and your breasts said another.

Last night we cooked up fish.

Last night the bass from two doors along
clashed with my own pulse.

Last night was filled with horsebones.

Last night was filled with temptation.

Last night; books remained unread,
the journal remained unwritten.

Last night we talked in the adverts
and skirted around ourselves.

Last night the cupboard contents engaged
in their daily miracle of becoming washing up.
The reversal is a task for Sisyphus,
rolling the stone.

Last night the devil in one eye,
a narrative in the other.

Last night. Light the candles. Flavour the room.
Move the walls closer. Tread the carpet.
Place knives down on the table, touch the bakelite years.
Dull clunk. Entering.

PINS & NEEDLES

That bed, spread with colour like a Klimt kiss.
We are wrapped in cloth, wrapped in glist.
Bound up with each other. Jigsaw pieces of arms.

You find me down the side of the couch.
You sleep hard on my chest. It only takes a minute.
Your breath in time with my heartbeat, and you sleep.

I watch & guess the light through the blind cracks.

In the steep field opposite cows are sleeping,
huddled together. A warm black and white chin
steams on another's back.

We are wrapped in purple and gold thread.
You wanted to feel royal. My chin against your forehead,
my sleeping arm quite numb & dead, holding round your back.

SKANDA-KARRITKEYA

War rides in to town as a peacock.
All his eyes on fire. Oil mixing with rain.

Peacock says: "This is my land.
This is my oil. This is my food."

We stand & fall in love. Fascinated, hypnotised,
separated by the blue flaming fire of the bird.
His colours brighter than a wedding kameez.
We cover our ears at his siren of a cry,
it does not stop his voice.

A small boy, all ribs & arms & legs kills the bird
by turning his back on it.
Tonight we share bread and feast for Eid.

ANNA

Fun Loving Criminals were playing on my ex's stereo.

Her flatmate Anna came home.

All the horniness in all the world charged me
like a Duracell. Made a mag lite of my eyes.
A heat seeking missile of my skin.
Every fluid nerve of me zoned & hot & embarrassed.

Running around all whacked up on scooby snacks.

Hello, I said, before losing all power of speech.

Everything was wrong. No satisfaction anywhere.
I never let on, but my skin burned day and night
for a taste of her.

CHRISTINE'S HAND

I have never been there.
Nor would I go now.
Not if you pack me a lunch
and fix the road for me.

A six mile hill leading back to you.
I've driven down it a couple of times
a week, but I've never been there.

There's a reservoir, burning alpines,
exploding purples caught in the swailing.
Walking knee deep in flowers & flames.
Kissed hot, melted, cooked away.

The palm of your hand; a six mile hill,
I would know every curve of this Pennine road,
the ring on your finger.
I've never been there.

NO MORE

No more of your kisses, your skin, your deep heat.
No more of our conversations, your hands, your eyes.

No more of this journey, this path, your thinking.
No more of your belly, your face, your flowering, your kisses.

Each day there is more missing. I wait by
the door for a letter, the computer
for an email, the phone for a text.
Each song singing itself on my radio
sings of you....And the planes of trees moving
in the wind talk of you. Even the ducks
in the park are in couples. There is more
and more. No more.

90 DAY THEORY

Day 91 as you kiss me, & your hand tugs at my fly.
A finger finding its way between my buttons bringing
lightning. Unfolding, lengthening me.

Three months of breathless horn.
Risks taken in alleys, cinema seats.
Dangerously perilous encounters with the gear stick.
Torn buttons. High collars at work.

Swooping along, this is it. Always thinking. Arriving tumescent.
Each thought a stroke on skin.

Day 91 as you kiss me & your hand grasps at my fly.
The couch creaks & the red crisp packet slides to the floor.
I keep one eye on the telly. Notice where the remote
falls down the side of the cushion. I know it is not going to be you.

We'll draw it out for a couple more months, before one
of us is honest or bored. Push faster to cum.
Find the smell of the carpet fusty. A whisper in me hopes
you won't notice that something in me has covered over.

HILLSIDE TRANSFORMATION

Our heavy feet
stumble, startling deer.
Climbing the hill
we struggle with. With light leaps,
perfect muscular explosions.

Their brown merging with the fern.
They stop to watch us through shrub.
Their stillness creates rock.

We watch each other
each with the right to be.
This becomes a prayer.

We know each other
on these skylines.
Each other's fear on display.
My head turns with antlers and
muscular neck to face my companion.
Deer's face to man's face
with the turn of a head.

CHERRY TREE

We are carving wood together,
I turn the head and Chris shapes with each beat.

The room is filled with cherry scent & schoolboys.
Every moment is its own. There is no talking,
no cause of pain.

I can smell the patchouli oil she wears.
We operate as one. I wonder do the schoolboys
notice our oneness. They are quiet too
shaping the pieces, rasping and smoothing,
carving shape. Constantly running their hands
over the limbs forming from each stroke and beat.

THE 159 FROM BRIXTON

for Martin Glynn

They turn up eventually. Those years like British transport.
It's been so long you didn't know you were waiting anymore.
It got to the point where you'd just lit a cigarette, then it
comes round the corner.

You're a school kid again. Forced to the upper deck. Seeing
things from a higher perspective through plasticky scratched
windows which read like swearing MUFC, MCFC.

Those years which you always hoped would never come,
though you didn't even realize you were hoping.
Your sister, brother, friend or mother dies and you go quiet.
It's one of those years where death visits nearly everyone
you know, in some way. You go quiet inside, and in the body.
Then your someone leaves unable to find enough of you
to touch anymore,

or it might be the other way round. They leave because
you've gone somewhere less fluorescent. Then the deaths
roll in.

You lie on the couch. The gas fire hissing, trying to take
the edge off. Friends have become satellites. Moving
in space. Doing their jobs. Sending you signals and txts
@ the WKEND. Silently orbiting your earth in the week,
busy with stellar tasks.

From the upstairs deck, where JENNA wz HERE, among
the rolling coke tin and the ads for telecom services, personal
loans and insurance, you get a great view.

VARIOLA

When I was a child I would study your face
lying on your chest, three years old, tracing
the long underside of your jawbone.
I am older than you now in your wedding pictures,
you are so boyish, that heavy madman's brow
like Lon Chaney - the Wolfman, black eyes.

Your slim body and those massive hands. I don't remember
being held by them, but I remember your face
the tender flesh pushed in by my boy fingers
moulding your cheek, your nose, round those eyes.

Your skin pockmarked as a golf ball.
Your face is a story you never told
me except it was smallpox.
You never spoke of the road to Pakistan,
the loss of everything, the journey
to Europe. I make those journeys but I don't know
where you go.

The gangly boy holding your sister's head.
The smooth skinned hands holding their heads
like nursing a baby. A whole family set on the road.
My father's three sisters, my Aunties. Maybe its right
that your names have been taken by the Punjabi
night sky. A heavy blanket of constellations.
Fat full moon watching you fall.

To the future produced by your fall.

No cloth of dreams. The impatient cries of three girls,
11, 12, & 13. The road sweeps by their last breath.
The cement trucks & the overladen
buses sweep by where their names were lost
they are only remembered by the dead now.

Eyes on the road
Mule loaded backs
Without thinking
With burning feet
Failing hands

three girls fall within days of each other
Survived by their parents
& their brothers
Mohammed & Rafiq
Eyes to the North
Loaded hearts
Without thinking too much
Pushing to the sea
Extinguish the burning
Becoming legal in Germany
The lost man in the photos
Working a way to England
The lost boy in his face

Without a permit they cross the borders
The border of scar tissue
Of a silent tongue
Of missing family
Of divided country
Of a promise of a common wealth
Of variola major
Of language
Of money
Of race
Of fear
Those eyes like the wolfman
The gate splintered
The boundary of scar tissue
Of silent tongue
Of three lost futures
three more stars for the cloth
Of three lost sisters
Of three lost names
Of lives who would have had families
Of paths that have been fenced and border patrolled
Of you & I & the living & the dead & politics
& war & ideas of nation & a country & a continent,
and, and, and I want to know something.
I want to know the stories, before and now, and I see
the borders in your eyes and it is for you to step into my country.

SIMPLE ECONOMICS

We will work
where they will not.

We will learn
where they refuse.

They talk amongst themselves,
say we steal their jobs.

They talk,
we work.

NECKGRIP

After the funeral
I found a box of photos.

My mum had only ever shown me
old polaroids my dad had taken
and her wedding album
                    full of the few
                    guests & had to be theres

ie. those who kept their thoughts,
about a black marrying a white woman,
behind their own curtains,

you might call it the presence of duty.

There are three photos in the box.
All of them portraits,
taken at some local photographer's studio.

The props of the 50's, almost Victoriana,
and my father in his best suit,
his neck and back rigid.
In one he is holding a brief case.
In another he is pictured with a radio.
In the last photograph it is just him,
standing against a dark curtained background
in his sharpest clothes:
all poses of affluence to be sent home
to give the impression of success.

At home I remember
my mum telling me
about having to work 12, 14 hours in the shop,
and the scraps she had to make meals with.

THE GOLDEN MILE

Playing the slots. Silver ten pences. Cherries,
nudges, a siren somewhere. Some day trip
all turned to rain. Haven't got any decent shoes.
My father takes us in to the amusements.

Radials of coloured bulbs, frying doughnuts.
He buys me a polystyrene tray of chips
with watery vinegar, and a tea which is all colour,
fake milk and grainy taste. I want to go on
the bumper cars. I watch the silver coins shove close
to the edge but never fall. Thump it hard with the flat
of my hand, give it a dig with my knee.
The grappler arm falls and I pray to get the shining watch.

ROOM FOR THE INVENTED FATHER

His walls are plain.
The colour of the room
quilted from book spines.

A sense of ozone.

Comfortable, but not opulent.
His pictures; abstract joy and found things.

A couch of welcome.
A table of manners.
The window reaches over the year,
as it changes, as I observe him,
push against him,
am like him.

The love and pulse of Miles, Coltrane,
Sonny Rollins, Sonny LeRoi,
change from goose honks to the story of ourselves.

And his chair, like a sea captain's or a poet's.
His back mapped into the leather.
His mixture of pipe smoke,
and his autumn in the woodsness.

This room is lived yet immaculate.
Amber nut wood floor
shining from its washings and
our stockinged feet.

CHEAP MOISTURISER

I worry every time I see her it may be
the last time. My mother is 74 this year,
that age when, if she doesn't answer
the phone, my stomach backspins.

Today I massaged her hands with moisturiser,
with drops of lavender mixed in it. Her arthritis
is really bad in her left hand. The thumb
closing over the palm. Her middle finger
thick ropey gristle beneath tissue transparent skin.

This is the first time we've done such a thing.
Mother objects at first, but begins to enjoy
my fingers pressing her fingers; the muscle-root
in her forearm, the small marbles that roll
across the muscle.

Often these days we dance to Abba or Queen,
quick two minute waltzes on her green cat-haired
rug that's always crooked. She's not been touched
much in her life. I die if a day goes by without a love.

She never hugged us once we'd stopped being small.
My sisters and I are knotty trees in
mum's garden. Now I try to feed and care
for her with lavender oil and hands, hoping
some of the love I taught myself will soak
into her fingers, and backflow into
her body, through the fibres she has grown
over her untouched desire.

BELFAST

Only when you look down at the corner kerbstones
painted red, white & blue, or green, white & yellow,
do you, the outsider, know you've wandered into a territorial war.

St. Roses School on the Falls Road, black fenced and razor
wired. A garden of the Virgin's Sacred Heart on the inside.
Girls being girls, playing and calling, in perfect grey uniforms.

I walk where no bus or taxi will go. Buggle eyed at the lack
of difference. A bright wall filled with a fearless red hand.
A mural opposite for patron saint Bobby Sands.

Here my brown skin is my advantage.
At night on the street boys with their girls are not afraid
to look you in the eye without being leery.
I can walk into town with no fear. They go about
their own business.

A squall of noise from the Empire bar. We drink the black stuff
and talk of choral voices and great books. When the empty glass
hits the table it is magically refilled. And we talk and talk.

Full breakfast of Denny's bacon. I go where I want,
and it's all the same: the talking, the love of life,
the books, the fences, the cornerstones.

The hush that surrounds each thing would eat me down
in one gulp if I looked too close. The wide lawns of Queen's.
The road out to Newcastle and the Mountains of Mourne.

The Green Man unthreads his roots, edging a tight hedge
about the city. He is patient. The docks with the crane's beaks
no longer feeding and dipping.

The burnt-out Ardoyne gives way to chickweed and grasses.
The green poking through the red, white and blue. Time slips,
a falling wine glass just about to hit the floor, its breaking
caught between silences.

I HATE TO ASK

One sock up and one sock down.
Pride and embarrassment on skinny brown legs.
Hidden under Marks and Spencer's charcoal school range.
Tiny knotted ties or huge wide inflated windsors.

The benches lined and filed for territorial games,
graded from sports and house captains,
down to Top Trump playing misfits.
White blouses. A hot neck. Ferrari beats Alfa Romeo.

I knew nothing but Abba and Billy Don't Be A Hero.
Drifted to mum's Roy Orbison 45s. At lunch
I could see but I did not understand. Are Friends
Electric?

Breaking my unquiet in my box room bedroom,
with the power-chords of Freebird and Saxon. Riffs
carried home on air guitar.

AFTER THE WEDDING

I am my father's will over my mother's acceptance of her life.
Her sparrow of wishes broken in flight by her own ignorance
and tutelage.

I was not planned when they married. He took her,
that's how it is. The street of my conception now laid
wide with tarmac and dispensable industrial units,
ringing corrugated roofed bells. Reflective metal spaces.

I would have liked to have been born of love instead of unknowing,
in meaningful sex, in heat, passion. Not giving and being taken.

Their world is too much of too little for me. These Xs and Ys.
This reckoning soul keeps doing the balances and misses
them both somehow.

FIFTYFIRSTSECOND

In the heaviest hush,
clothes become transparent.
Fruit washes down.
Hair plastered to face.
Arms holding myself.
Arms not reaching far enough.
Arms touching tree bark,
drops on fingers,
bigger feeling/extra texture.

Arms cold with wet cloth,
       with goosepimples.
       Hearing the noise cut down the traffic,
       with the itch of eczema cooling.

Arms trying to keep a man dry
       wiping water and salt away.
Arms thinking of lost sons;
       a court case,
       a miscarriage,
       and one other.
Arms against law,
deep in the kidneys,
shopping bag plastic holds and cuts three fingers.
Arms walk home.
       Ask tree of life.
       Ask tree of knowledge.
Arms feel the headache coming,
in waves with the sound.
Each sound hurts
in the spine and the mind.
Arms cover my head.
Arms cover my head.
       They pump petrol.
       They bear the arms of initiation.
       Carry tattoos of many fingers.

Dry elbow skin against nylon,
forgot to get cream.

Arms ask in rituals for a god.
        In their muscle lines a totem.
        In their nerves an idea of how to see.

Arms rubbed dry with towel.
        Stiff in all their holding.

Arms rest on table.
        Talk their own way.
        Won't stay hidden.

THE SEA

based on LS Lowry's painting "The Sea"

No towers of stone.
No landmass.
No you or me.

No pier,
or dogs,
or thoughts of rent collecting.

Overcast
sea and sky meet in a moving edge,
it rolls back and forward,
takes the hardness away.

In the music.
God in the spaces.
In the sea,
ebbed into spaces.

I become the sea wall
and the wave.
I have the cloud and the light,

let the power fall,
I will hold nothing.

The sea is each breathing.
Each breath is colourless,
it moves the spine
and opens the front.

No landmass.
No tower.
No I.

THE PRIZE

Now I am blind
I see you.

Now I am deaf
I can hear your love.

Now that my teeth are gone,
I want to taste your meat.

Now that the daylight is short
I live in your light.

Frailty calls at the door everyday,
he is my company and sounding board,
I tell him of the strength I feel inside.

They cleared the wood to
grow a forest.

The bombs I set
bloom in blood shades,
give pleasure in the garden.

The great impact will come
in forgetfulness
when the silences accumulate.

DIAMONDS

Doorbells ring in elsewhere,
pencils well defined.
This skyline is far from beautiful.
Each window lacks an optimism,
that once had the energy of a bees nest,
a hexagonal wax life-tube,
royal jelly is denied to create drones.
The dance is sacred to their way of life,
no one questions the bees.

The fluorescents hum,
no apologies, at least they
coldly do their job.

Passing through circles
a wrist bends.
Feet take their weight.
Some process is stuck in her mind.
The speaker is too quiet on its stand.

On his mountain,
a song of unknown words.
Let them talk amongst themselves.
I can whistle and hum at the same time.
I taste coffee and know its cheap stuff,
worry about everything.
See pharaohs on thrones in hot places,
walk into a wood and try to find
home;
in the green filter,
in the smoker's cough,
in the cutting of wood,
in the song and rhythms of daily work.

Don't know what my job is anymore,
abstract from subsistence's pleasures.
Work has become overly defined
as a way to feed the machine.
In the woods, I believe again.
Each little nature god can undo me.

Each vision of a church of greens,
but I say to myself,
got to.
Got to.
Got to,

and the morning's coffee mixes with the
taste of fear in my mouth,
and the morning's coffee mixes with the fear of insects,
and the morning's coffee mixes with the fear of letting it all fall,

in the Dharmakaya,
the blue bliss bodies of Buddhas,
there is a door which opens to all possibility.

I wanna kick my way through rooms,
waggle my bum in the face of landlords,
then eat a huge breakfast at a greasy joe's.

Plants grow around my legs,
I have stood still and am covered in your ivy.

John Coltrane's soul-bop
is the gardener that commits topiary
on these hedges.
Fractal cuts, beyond shape
repeating down.
All in the math of the world.
All in the mouth of me.
Teeth edges in sleep,
see through your smiles.

Behind your face are some lights,
scared of insects.
John says don't sweat it
and throws my entrails and thoughts
into zen math,
through open window
back to be,
plant man.
Bee man.
Song man.
Man man.
A little fire.

SEASCAPE

The breath comes closer now.

The air darker now,

and all my love is in front of me,
all my beloved who I never told.

Grass in a field.
Field in the open air.
Airflow,
down I go
churning bowels.

Opening and churning me.

It is quiet here.
Is this what I am?

The all I see is my hands.
The opium
cracking.
Will you know me
stripped down?

Will you love me still?
Is it too late to guess?

The road I fell in love with.
The red of my old car,
driven to the end.
Down is the sea,
lying with heads on the ground.
The sucking water
          has speech in it
                    it says
the wheel,
the wheel.

Lift my small wings
out,
over.
Rolling away from the land,
picking small thermals out.
It is in the air
that
          moment
I always tried
                    to
speak of.

OMBRE

Her hair is a church.
Opening his guts to
worship at her.
To brush his hands
over her head.
To kiss her there
and there.

Kissing crowns,
lost in all but softness.
Shampoo compulsion - dizzy,
remembering all that should
have been.
All he ever wanted in woman.

THE FUNERAL PARTY

Mother's death
plays
over and over glitching
with each skip,
half a line of a song
locked with an off beat.

Locked groove worn
into the eyes.
She is a small cold bird.
Must ring work to tell them.

How long does it take to function?
How long does it take to crack?
Everything is inappropriate,
even a New Orleans jazz party
would break our hearts.

We are a picture
lost and ridiculous in tight ties
and mothballed coats.

IN A WARDROBE OF PLEASURE

There is a fire inside all wood.
The essence of wood smoke
always a potential.

Shirts breathe in this.

A boy under windless washing.

A spaceship. A quiet
for my head.

Mother's cursing of " I don't effin
swear," at my sister, reduced
to the idea of motion.

The toe of a shoe
wedged into my back, stops
the sleep passing through.

Ideas of parallax and plants
tumble in the unfocusable
darkness.

Deep space.
Under belts and ties,
unlit sky.

The ship moves beyond
our galaxy, where there
are few stars. Where

gases are measured in millionths.

AN EAGLE IS STRUCK BY MADNESS

Three cogs that change nothing.
Four heads empty of self.
FORGET YOUR PAST.
Your heritage is irrelevant.
New York. New Babel.
Oh God, I lived it twice.
Three towers hold black the sky.

Three funnels drink the rain.
A ladder whose first rung
cannot be reached.
Camshaft - I am driven.
Subway - consume.
New Theatre - consume.
Engine - consumed.

When I am
Educated, Educated, Educated,
there will be:
community, identity, stability.

On the subway roof
a brown feather.
In the black sky -
no bird.

BELIEVABLE

If there had been a crash.

If I had a virus.

If my legs, arms neck were broken.

If I had been stabbed or shot.

If I'd been beaten.

If I'd been mugged.

If I'd been burnt in fire.

If a building had fallen on me.

Then you might believe
I am ill.

FULL UP

Silence beside the couch,
under the bed.
Silence in the pockets
of jackets hanging together.
Silence behind the television,
in the place that is never vacuumed.

I am silent in the kitchen,
over a tin of beans and sausages.

I am silent at home.

She fills everything,
this silent woman.
She is so full, she is shouting,
I move quietly.

ISOLATED INCIDENTS

A wheat field.

A red car set amongst
white grid of asphalt car park.

Stars separated
by numbers we can say,
by distances we cannot live.

Shining plastic of a cheap pen
not moved, all those stories
kept in waiting.

Minds held in wishes to connect.

The sun comes up and goes down
on her loss.

Photos held in memory.
Memory held in skin.
Skin once loved by hands.
Hands that caressed sweet love.

Love shines on.
Love remains.
His face is getting younger by the day.

Her photos change meaning
with each explanation.

No explanation for the distance
in the universe, still moving apart.

No explanation in the distance
in conversation, which changes
with the channels as she fingers
the remote.

An empty coat peg.

A day from before
which is better than all these years.

A lid of a pickle jar
too tight to move.
She craves his hand to touch.
She craves his strength now,
as she places the jar
back in the cupboard.

Keeping a plate, a cup,
a knife, fork, spoon and teaspoon,
and a bowl,
always set out for herself.

Always washing up her set
immediately after her small tea
of Krackawheat, lettuce,
Dairylea, tomato, ham,
and tonight no pickle.

THE STOLEN

I would reach out a hand to take my son's hand.
I would swivel a knee to dandle him.

Like calling through a fog,
caught in the deep grass which quickens
round my legs up here at the top of creation.

I would pass the years through a gold skimming pan,
picking out the flecks for the rush.

I would reach my hand across the years
to find his arm to pick him up.

Hard bread for the palate. Liquid, too hot for the lips.
A map of a demolished town.

I would melt the gold like the fool I am. Spread the leaf
over stones and leaves. I might plate the breadth of England,
and still find myself wanting to reach him, without a clue
of what I would say.

THE DANGER & RESULT OF DAYS SPENT WITH A NARROWING MIND, REPETITION, WAGE SLAVERY & CONSERVATISM

Bored
of a day like another day.

Riskless
now in life,
a motorway to a grave.

You're eating sandwiches
from the devil's lunch box.

A TIME IN THE SOUTH PACIFIC NO.7

One time in the south pacific
we sat as rocks,
immobile with heads like flowers
made of tiny shells.

I am bound to you by raffia like emotion.
I am bound into the parcel of myself.

Bound tobacco leaves,
guarded by fierce pearls.

Kept in two bundles.
This wish, to be a cigarette with you
burning for five minutes,
then the closed doors won't matter
anymore.

Our nicotine will yellowly line
the ceiling and walls,
        and no one will know.

DEEP BLUE DAY

for Andy Kearney

It seems like a long time
since I held you.

Do you remember when we both
fell in love with the daffodils
your lover had brought you?

Flat on our backs from too much something
yellow fountaining out into gold,
& we ate bread and honey.

Singing impromptu country & western songs
when we ran out of words,
we'd just string swearing together,
'Oh mah daahlin.'

We'd be brothers forever.
Time's laughing her socks off now,
we've drifted.

I have a memory & a heartspace
for a brother.

The hills around our town are
the buffalo plains of imagining.

Our guitar twanging is still out there
like perfume, it sings me to sleep.

Elvis is on the radio,
      "If there's one thing she don't need
        it's another hungry mouth to feed

          in the ghetto."

PERFUME

O with the smell of oil and flowers.

With samarkand and sandalwood anoint me.

Bathe deep in rose water,

and walk as shimmering light
dappled on the ground
                everywhere.

There must be incense,
this serpent loves the smell.

Plait flowers for me.

With betel leaf reddening your lips,
kiss me,
    kiss me.

COMPRESSION

Waited through the light no-light
to be born.

Waited for self consciousness,
sewing sparking moments together,
not knowing the length of summer.

Waited to be older.

Waited for mother's respect.

Waited to find your lover.

Maybe when ten years have passed
you can quit the job.

Paid off the house.

Found your hair to be grey.

Waited for the law to bring justice.

For this country to be fair.

For it to be a happier world.

Watched them grow bigger than you.

Waited for the visit.

Waited in the blue chair
and the room with your pictures in.
A long wait,
watching the soaps,
small trips out,
talked to like a child.
Not asked about the design of engines,
or the future,
or the movement and pattern of things.

The last wait,
a long weight
free of variety.

Waited through the layering down.

Waited in the light no-light.

There is something
waiting in potential.

THOUGHTS YOU WOULD BE
EMBARRASSED BY #1

Some people really want the world
to be a beautiful place,
they make consistent efforts
pruning and mowing and even
making a flowerbed
by the side of the road
with bricks, soil and cuttings
from their own garden.

Where before it was just dusty pink gravel,
there is clematis,
and some plants whose names I don't know.

She goes inside to admire her work
from the window.
Catches her son's eye in a photo
on her way to the kitchen,
washes the soil from her hands,
and goes outside to continue her memory.
The tree was a lot smaller then.

She hears the sound of play and looks
over the garden wall,
and thinks Paki bastards
at the 4 and 5 year old kids playing house.

BOXED IN

I've forgotten so many words recently
since death came to visit our house.
Words seem to be pennies for the eyes.

There are things which I make out I forget
but never can. The shitty hole of the town
I came from. Another life as an electrical engineer.

I've forgotten what a first date feels like.
Marriage's cool tracks may be the journey,
often it is the beginnings which excite the traveller.

I've forgotten the sounds of life before the age of 5.
Memories run like Charlie Chaplin films,
a title card and grainy light.

I've forgotten
why work is so important.

I've forgotten to forget. Became an old cupboard
with several lonely shoes, a stack of jigsaws and board-games,
an electric meter, gardening clothes and a box of matches.

TO WRITING

Until you came I had no voice of my own, I would
borrow song lyrics for my feelings, use films as examples.
Struggle for words. Always. Always.

Before you came, I was an illiterate marking an x instead
of saying my name. Face down in shame. Always outcaste.

I throw myself into you, an unrequited
lover, expecting all the rewards I had dreamed, maybe
even a taste of the unnameable things, but you
are not love, though you are my one and only.
Showing me treasure. Feeding me with so many stories.

When the poem is over, the audience leaves, its just
you and me again.

THOUGHT

Always the refuge, never the answer. A field
full of play where the ball is never thrown. I have
crossed your border. Asked for asylum in your country.
I am your detainee, proving my case.
Telling the politics and position of my homeland.

You are my food coupons in Safeway, pretending
to be money in my hand. You are thought to be
the difference between anarchy and civilisation. I am tired
of thinking of you, thought. You are not meat, or bread,
or the body, you are not enough to live by.

I was wrong to come here, an economic
exile. Deport me back. Show me as a scrounger
in the paper. Put me under armed guard and march
me to the next plane to the physical.
Maybe you can use me as an anecdote
down the pub when I'm gone.

YES

Yes to the Martian canals that run the length of me. Yes to the frozen lakes beneath my fields. Yes to yes. Yes to my atomic self. Yes to the lover. Yes to the tarot card playing fool with poker face believing this means something. Yes to stardust, I am fleshed by you. Yes to perspiration, sweat, labour, working with my hands. Yes to the dancing self that gets pissed and pisses in the long grass, writing its name with hot splash. Yes I am the same dust as you. Yes to my soul. Yes to my death, I hope I never loose sight of you. Yes to breathing which makes my dust a body, so I can hate & cry & make love & fuck, fuck, fuck. Yes to falling on the floor crying my heart out. Yes to having a heart to cry. Yes to the hand that can write yes. Yes to yes.

SUCKING THE MANGO

Bare the mast,
press hard.

Be passionate while I'm half inside,

and suck and press and
raise your tongue.

The cool skin of a mango
opens into orange wetness.
The strange stone pushes
the softness back.

STRAWBERRIES

From the first day, we talked.
Our first real meeting, talking, eating
strawberries in the park. You were leaving
your job. This was your little goodbye party,
it was just the two of us, everyone else faded
into the scene. A big bowl of strawberries
& us & the future. Talking.

We always talk. We can go for days.
These are real conversations, not just waiting
for the other to stop so we can say the next
fixed clever thing. Even after years
there is much to say. Our marriage is built from talking,
the witnesses are dolmen, we change our minds
on the altar cloth of discussion, it's how we become
who we are.

I can tell by the way the leaves dance & the windows
shine, that god is pleased with us.
We talk to keep ourselves clean.

SACRAMENT

On your wedding day, I shall hold a funeral
for the lives you have closed.

I shall bury you, place a headstone
above you, leaving it blank except
for your photo there for anyone to see
how lovely your were in life.

PACKING FOR THE AFTERLIFE

Sitting on an astral suitcase, its side
bulging with solutions, trying to pre-empt
forever's needs. Is there a future

in the afterlife? Maybe my packing
shouldn't be so linear. I'll take out
the alarm clock, give myself up to whatever.

Don't need a thong in heaven, they can go too.
I'd rather hang free for eternity. Forget all this stuff.
I'll take a couple of Coltrane CDs,
to use as maps of the infinite. The photo album
is a must, in death love can be lived more equally,
I can say all your names again.

It would be much easier if I were a pharaoh,
just take everyone and everything.

The great pyramids of West Yorkshire,
the ninth wonder of the world.

MANJI

Hold the rosary through the fire of the mind.
Hold the spirit, through the broken heart.
Hold compassion, even against your will.

Hold the phases of the moon in your hand.
Hold the water of the sea in your tears.
Hold the drop of love that still holds on.

Hold the loneliness as it bites.
Hold your own hand on the Godforsaken days.
Hold your will, when your body fails.

In your tears there is a seed.
In this seed there is your soul.
In your soul there is a friend.
In this friend you see yourself.
The universe turns inside out like a wild horse.
Heave your heart to the wild horse.
The earth, the sky, the six directions.

The four phases of the moon draw your tide.
The leviathans dive deep in your gravity.
Hold the monsters as they call your name.
Hold your name as they call your shame.
Hold the moon in your cupped hands.

WANTING

I used to tie my hair back to show my face,
I didn't know you then. I don't know you now.

I would wear my jeans still damp off the line
in the rush to go and meet you.

I can't tie my hair back anymore, I'm all face.
Tom Waits is singing '….one tattooed tear
for every year he's away.'

I didn't know you then. You look older to me now,
without the eyes of love to smooth you out.

You're dressed in Marks & Spencer.
With me you'd have dressed in red.

I want to tie my hair back to show my face.
Damp jeans rushing to meet you. Without the eyes
of love to sing, one for every year.

THE MORNING ANGELUS

Orange cats drinking water from a rain filled enamelled
tin bowl. Herb Rocket gone to flower on a windowsill,
becoming droopy, overlong, with seed making.
A hot bath with no one else in the house.

Good paper, strong black coffee, no thought of religion
or getting it right. Making lists while the turning of the record
plays a piano sonata, giving space between its notes.

We would call for each other, when we were boys, go out
on missions, climb around in building sites, walk or cycle
on our chopper bikes to the moors, the iron waters, drink
the red water. Feet on the cold stone, polished.

A MIDDAY ANGELUS

I want to walk until I have no name.
To have to sit down on a small road
in a shallow valley somewhere, with low purple
alpine flowers behind me, grasshoppers mixing
up sound, and the pale silver undersides
of leaves revealing the coming rain,
their tough veins keeping out the direct sun.

With no name, with no double life, no inner,
no outer, no explanations, I celebrate not knowing,
not having to be somebody. I celebrate my skin,
and the sun darkening it, while my inside is like
those undersides of leaves. Where there is a back,
there is always a front. A leaf has two sides
and it is one leaf.

Rough horsetails for my bed. A church bell calls
the hours. The grasshoppers' chirps intensify
with the sun moving out of cloud. I celebrate
the underside. I celebrate all those things
that go unsaid. I celebrate not playing along,
being bored of conversation. The sky can take me.
A flash of silver glimpsed when the wind blows up.

THE EVENING ANGELUS

Eating an onion as if it's an apple
every day to keep out the cold, to clean the blood.
You're alone in your work, before the war.
Wearing a shirt and tie beneath blue overalls
to garden in the park.

I knew you would stand like that, a small Irish reservoir dog.
Trowelling hands, laying out Italian marigolds for the summer.
Scything fingers cutting gladioli
for your youngest, Norah. You have no idea about what's coming.

Handing your wage packet to Katherine
every Friday night. Falling asleep in your chair
near the kitchen fire, before she bosses you
out to work on the house. She'll be gone in twenty years,

your eight children will become seven, and you
will move to the mill lands of Northern England.
You love your job, the quiet soil, dirty nails.
You were your own man five days a week,
Kate's in the evening, mine somewhere ahead of you.

UTTAR PRADESH 1977

The Volvo glows maximum red.
Even the long sundowning shadows fear it,
they fall to the side rather than darken its paintwork.

Red like it's ready to go. An instant relief
from the sand that colours everything; cloth, ground and air.

A barefoot man in glasses, wrapped in browns,
his hand and his head, loose with waiting.
Gone so far beyond patience to beg a ride
from the car's owner, his blood has pooled into numb stillness.
He sits by the door on the driver's side
leaning his vertebrae open to the edge of the sill,
as if his spine has always been part of the car.

The tents of the mela emptying.
Denim hanging on willow poles.
The food stalls gone. The dogs rummaging.

If I were to ask him to stand, make him some chai,
he wouldn't move. He is as much a part of this place
as the small stones that whip up in the breeze to chip
long bare galvanised scratches in extreme red,
that have to be buffed out to maintain glorious pride.

DENMARK STREET FURNITURE

The mirror is the only thing
that is left after my father has gone.

It hangs above the glowing gas fire
which hisses its breath to warm the room.

The mirror reflects everything in the room,
ourselves in chairs, tiny flowers in the wallpaper.

Its bevelled edge folding the light.
We sit in dark not connected to the past.

The standard lamp, 60W bulb, pools
a yellow circle, an island at its foot.

VESPERS AT SACRE COEUR

Nuns singing against the patterning
dulcimer under the blue dome.

The blue dome sending their song in swirls
around the church walls.

I light a candle, naming the past
in a head-whisper.

All gods lead to god, all gods lead away
from god – I have no redeemer.

The prayer from my heart is the centre
of this flame, the singing in the dome.

Not of the words, but the flame and the sound.
Not in the burning, but in the light

and the darkness around it, not in the song,
but the wave that comes just after,

the hope in each believer. Not in the god,
but in the believing. Not in the words

but in the faith. No redeemer, not one
is born in sin, but it is in the sinning that

we lose ourselves and learn to lie, learning
to sit still. The wave that follows the sound.

The image that comes after the candle.
The footfall that comes from not moving.
I have found you there outside of names.

I came to pray, and I prayed, made offerings,
sat in the hard chairs. Nothing beats the heart

but the heart's own beating. It is in the not
listening that we have become liars.

It is in the loss of the nameless
that we have named. In the need to be redeemed

we are lost. In the need for security
we become housebound. No gods lead to god.

No saviour brings us back. It's the heart's beating
in the darkness, in the aftershock, in the letting slip
of names, in the straying from the path,
in the losing of hope; the heart still beats.

SELF-PORTRAIT, JUNE 2004, JALHANDAR

I always thought I'd pose naked for this.
I came as a picture, light woollen dark
suit, precise with details to throw off
the expected, Indian shirt, cheap silver
earrings, one grey chest hair, like the first fallen leaf
in autumn, predicting the shedding soon to follow.

My parents are at the window. The woodwork
is peeling to show dark red, this room could be
deep and beautiful if it wasn't for its paper and paint.

Four weeks of Weight–Watchers before I stand
in front of this mirror, with only three slips
in that time, fish & chips, a big kebab,
and one night a keema dosa cooked on the street
and eaten before anyone could see.

In the mirror our eyes shine at each other,
he smiles expecting me to be his boy again,
my hair has gone, like his. Mother is doing
her angry/quiet face. They both stand
on a milk crate to see me better.

The suit of my defence hides a belly I've always hated.
Under the clothes of poet I grasp for language
like a poor swimmer; for my lack of symmetry,
one eye higher than the other, the blue of beard shadow.

I choose gouache and cubist strokes to try to demonstrate
my movement away from their eyes. The biggest change
is in my cheeks, now a bit jowly from my fried chicken habit.

Jalhandar's gardens have meaty dark leaves.
Rousseau's tiger is in the trees. My socks are old
and don't match the blue wool. I can paint
what I like: the fleshy leaves, the family eyes.

John Siddique was born in Rochdale, Lancashire, in 1964. His mother was from Northern Ireland, his father's family had left India during the Partition and his father came to Europe by way of Pakistan. Rochdale 'was a very difficult place to be a child', and he left as soon as he was able, moving to Northern Ireland and then to Manchester. He currently lives in West Yorkshire. After school he did various jobs, including a three year stint as a landscape gardener. He started writing in 1991, when he was 27. He has been involved in many writing and performing projects and posts including Poet in Residence at The Lowry, at Meadowbrook Psychiatric Unit, at Ilkley Literature Festival, and at BBC Manchester: he also worked for three years as Writer in Residence at Wetherby Prison. Between 1999 and 2003 he was Writer in Residence for Young People at the Ledbury Poetry Festival. He works as a Tutor for various organizations including the Arvon Foundation.